PRINCEWILL LAGANG

Prayerful Dating: Seeking God's Will in Relationships

First published by PRINCEWILL LAGANG 2023

Copyright © 2023 by Princewill Lagang

All rights reserved. No part of this publication may be reproduced, stored or transmitted in any form or by any means, electronic, mechanical, photocopying, recording, scanning, or otherwise without written permission from the publisher. It is illegal to copy this book, post it to a website, or distribute it by any other means without permission.

Princewill Lagang asserts the moral right to be identified as the author of this work.

First edition

This book was professionally typeset on Reedsy.
Find out more at reedsy.com

Contents

1	The Quest for Meaningful Connections	1
2	Foundations of Faith in "Prayerful Dating"	4
3	Discernment: Navigating the Path of God's Will	7
4	The Art of Communication and Connection	10
5	Nurturing a Relationship with God Together	13
6	Encountering Challenges on the Path	17
7	Celebrating Love in God's Will	20
8	Passing the Torch of Wisdom	23
9	A Lifetime of Love and Faith	27
10	The Journey Continues	30
11	A Love Story Written by God	33
12	A Lifetime of Gratitude	36

1

The Quest for Meaningful Connections

Title: "Prayerful Dating: Seeking God's Will in Relationships"

In the quiet of an early morning, as the first rays of sunlight paint the sky with delicate hues of pink and gold, we find ourselves at the beginning of a journey. A journey not merely through the pages of this book but through the intricate pathways of our hearts. It is a quest, a quest for love and companionship guided by the gentle hand of faith. This journey is one that millions have embarked upon, each with their unique dreams, desires, and experiences, but all seeking one thing above all else – God's will in their relationships.

The concept of "Prayerful Dating" may be unfamiliar to some, perhaps even counterintuitive to others. Dating is often seen as a worldly endeavor, an arena of personal choices and romantic pursuits that exist apart from religious or spiritual considerations. However, the essence of this book lies in the belief that faith and romance can, and should, coexist harmoniously. The heart, after all, is not just a vessel for emotion but a sacred chamber where God's guidance can be sought, even in matters of love.

But why "Prayerful Dating"? Why should we embark on this path, distinct from conventional dating approaches? To answer these questions, we must begin by exploring the world we live in and the profound changes that have shaped our approach to relationships in recent years.

The Modern Landscape of Love

In the digital age, the landscape of love and dating has undergone a seismic shift. From swiping right on dating apps to the instant gratification of online communication, our lives are more connected than ever, and yet many of us feel lonelier than before. We are bombarded with an abundance of choices, but amidst the noise, many find it challenging to discover deep and meaningful connections.

The fast-paced nature of modern dating can often lead to decisions based on impulse, infatuation, or even superficial judgments. The result is a generation that is yearning for something more, something that transcends fleeting moments and superficial encounters. A desire for a love that is built on a strong foundation, one that withstands the test of time and reflects the values we hold dear.

A Sacred Partnership

In "Prayerful Dating," we seek to address this longing. We believe in the possibility of cultivating relationships that are not only loving and lasting but are also reflective of our faith and the guidance of a higher power. This is a journey towards a sacred partnership where we recognize the divine presence in our lives, not only individually but also in the relationships we form.

But what exactly does "Prayerful Dating" entail, and how can we embark on this journey with an open heart and a faithful spirit? Throughout this book, we will explore the principles and practices of this unique approach to dating.

We will delve into the art of discernment, the significance of prayer, and the importance of self-reflection. We will uncover the ways in which our faith can enrich our relationships, making them not only sources of joy but also instruments for personal growth and spiritual fulfillment.

Finding Purpose in This Journey

Our journey into "Prayerful Dating" is not just about finding a partner but about discovering ourselves, understanding our values, and aligning our life choices with our faith. It's about realizing that the desire for love and companionship is not at odds with our spiritual beliefs but can be a channel for experiencing God's grace in a profound and beautiful way.

As we embark on this expedition, we encourage you to open your heart to the possibilities that lie ahead, to seek the wisdom of your faith, and to embrace the transformative power of prayer. Together, we will explore the foundations of "Prayerful Dating" and the practical steps you can take to embark on this meaningful and fulfilling journey towards finding God's will in your relationships.

In the pages that follow, we will uncover the importance of discernment, the art of listening, and the beauty of trust. "Prayerful Dating" is not a guarantee of a trouble-free journey, but it is an assurance that you will be walking hand in hand with your Creator, seeking His will in the sacred dance of love. So, let us embark on this journey together, open to the endless possibilities, and with unwavering faith in the belief that love, when approached with prayerful intent, can be a divine gift that leads us to greater spiritual heights.

Are you ready to begin your journey into "Prayerful Dating"? If so, let us step into the world of faith, love, and purpose, where the quest for meaningful connections unfolds before us like the petals of a blossoming rose.

2

Foundations of Faith in "Prayerful Dating"

Title: "Prayerful Dating: Seeking God's Will in Relationships"

In the quiet corners of our hearts, where our deepest convictions reside, lies the foundation upon which "Prayerful Dating" is built. This chapter delves into the essence of faith and its role in shaping our approach to relationships. Before we can embark on a journey seeking God's will, we must first understand the role of faith as our guiding star, illuminating the path towards meaningful connections.

The Power of Faith

Faith, as a fundamental aspect of our lives, extends its influence into every corner of our existence. It's the bedrock upon which we build our beliefs, values, and aspirations. In "Prayerful Dating," faith serves as the anchor that keeps us grounded amidst the tempestuous seas of modern romance. It is the belief that our Creator is intimately involved in our lives and desires the best for us.

Our faith tells us that we are not alone in this world, that our journey towards love is not a solitary one. We have a divine companion, a source of wisdom, love, and guidance. With faith, we find the strength to persevere when faced with challenges and the patience to wait for the right person and the right time.

Recognizing Divine Timing

One of the foundational principles of "Prayerful Dating" is the acknowledgment of divine timing. Faith teaches us that God's plans may not always align with our desires, but His timing is perfect. This recognition leads to a fundamental shift in perspective, encouraging us to trust the process and embrace the belief that God's plan is unfolding, even when it's not immediately evident to us.

"Prayerful Dating" invites us to relinquish the pressure of forcing a relationship to fit our own timelines. Instead, it encourages us to recognize that the right person will enter our lives when it's divinely ordained. This change in mindset allows us to approach dating with a sense of serenity and assurance that we are not chasing after love but waiting for it to find us.

The Role of Self-Reflection

Before we can fully understand the importance of faith in "Prayerful Dating," we must also consider the role of self-reflection. It is through introspection that we unearth our own beliefs, values, and goals. Self-reflection enables us to identify areas of our lives where faith plays a vital role, and it helps us discern how our faith aligns with our desires in the realm of relationships.

"Prayerful Dating" is not a passive process. It requires us to actively engage with ourselves and our beliefs. We must ask ourselves challenging questions: What does faith mean to me? How does it influence my life choices? Do my actions align with my beliefs? Through this self-examination, we not only strengthen our connection with faith but also prepare ourselves to engage in relationships guided by our convictions.

The Practice of Prayer

Central to "Prayerful Dating" is the practice of prayer. In the world of faith, prayer is our direct line of communication with the divine. It's the means by which we seek guidance, clarity, and strength. In the context of relationships, prayer becomes a powerful tool for seeking God's will.

Prayer enables us to lay our hopes, fears, and desires before our Creator, asking for His guidance and seeking His blessings. It allows us to release control and trust that God is actively working in our lives, even in matters of the heart. Through prayer, we become active participants in our journey towards love, seeking divine insight and nurturing a relationship with our Creator that enriches all aspects of our lives.

In the pages that follow, we will explore the practical aspects of incorporating faith and prayer into your dating journey. "Prayerful Dating" is not about relinquishing control; it's about inviting God to walk alongside you, guiding your steps and illuminating your path. Together, we will learn to trust in divine timing, embrace self-reflection, and seek guidance through prayer, all of which will lay the foundation for a dating experience that transcends the ordinary and becomes a sacred journey towards love and God's will in relationships.

3

Discernment: Navigating the Path of God's Will

Title: "Prayerful Dating: Seeking God's Will in Relationships"

As we continue our journey into "Prayerful Dating," we enter the realm of discernment. This chapter explores the art of discernment in the context of dating, guiding us to make choices that align with God's will. Discernment is the compass that keeps us on the path of purpose, ensuring that our relationships are not merely rooted in desire but also in the divine plan.

The Nature of Discernment

Discernment is a process of careful consideration, a journey of self-discovery guided by faith. In the context of dating, it serves as the bridge between the desire for companionship and the will of God. This is where we learn to distinguish between what our hearts long for and what God intends for us.

Discernment is a journey of seeking clarity, understanding, and wisdom. It enables us to recognize the signs and guidance that God places in our path, helping us make choices that lead us towards love that is in harmony with our faith.

Cultivating a Discerning Heart

To embark on the path of discernment in "Prayerful Dating," we must cultivate a discerning heart. This begins with self-awareness. We need to understand our own desires, values, and priorities. This self-knowledge becomes the foundation upon which we build our discernment process.

A discerning heart is also a humble heart, open to the possibility that our own desires may not always align with God's plan. It is a heart that acknowledges its limitations and is willing to submit to the divine will. This humility allows us to trust the process and believe that God's plan is unfolding, even when we don't fully comprehend it.

Seeking God's Guidance

At the heart of discernment is the act of seeking God's guidance. Through prayer and reflection, we invite God into our decision-making process. We lay our desires before Him, asking for His wisdom and clarity. We seek signs, inspiration, and peace in our hearts as we navigate the complex world of dating.

Discernment is a dynamic process. It requires us to be attentive to the signals and guidance God provides. These signals can come in many forms, such as a sense of peace, a feeling of unease, or even through the wisdom of trusted spiritual mentors. As we develop a discerning heart, we learn to recognize and interpret these signals with increasing accuracy.

Trusting the Process

Discernment is not always a straightforward or quick process. It requires patience and trust. There may be moments of confusion, doubt, or frustration. However, "Prayerful Dating" reminds us that the journey itself is as important as the destination.

Trust is essential. We must trust that God's plan for us is perfect, and even if it seems to take a winding path, it will ultimately lead us to where we are meant to be. This trust allows us to stay the course, even when faced with challenges or when the answers we seek remain elusive.

Applying Discernment in Dating

In the pages that follow, we will explore practical ways to apply discernment in your dating journey. We will delve into the importance of defining your relationship values, understanding the significance of red flags, and learning to listen to your intuition.

"Prayerful Dating" is not about perfection; it's about the process. It's about seeking God's will through discernment, trusting His guidance, and making choices that align with your faith. As you embrace discernment, you will find that your dating experience becomes not only purposeful but also spiritually enriching, guiding you towards relationships that are blessed by God's grace.

4

The Art of Communication and Connection

Title: "Prayerful Dating: Seeking God's Will in Relationships"

In our journey through "Prayerful Dating," we have explored the foundations of faith, the importance of discernment, and the role of prayer in seeking God's will. As we continue, we enter the realm of human interaction, where the intricate art of communication and connection takes center stage. This chapter delves into the significance of building meaningful relationships through open and purposeful communication.

The Language of Love

Communication is the lifeblood of any relationship. It's through conversation, both spoken and unspoken, that we get to know one another on a deeper level. In "Prayerful Dating," the art of communication is elevated to a spiritual practice. It becomes the means by which we seek understanding, nurture connection, and explore the potential for God's will to unfold in our relationships.

Effective communication is more than just talking; it's about listening, understanding, and connecting. It's about the exchange of thoughts, feelings, and beliefs. In this chapter, we explore how communication can become a vehicle for seeking God's will in your relationships.

The Role of Active Listening

Listening is an often overlooked aspect of communication. In "Prayerful Dating," we emphasize the significance of active listening as a way to honor your partner and seek God's guidance. Active listening means not merely hearing the words spoken but truly understanding the emotions, desires, and intentions behind those words.

By actively listening, you can discern the deeper layers of your partner's heart and soul. You can seek to understand their beliefs, values, and the role of faith in their life. Through this understanding, you can assess whether your relationship aligns with God's will and whether you can support each other's spiritual growth.

Transparent and Authentic Communication

Honesty is a core principle of "Prayerful Dating." It means sharing your thoughts, feelings, and beliefs openly and authentically. Honesty fosters trust and builds the foundation for a strong and meaningful connection. In a world where we often put on masks or hide our true selves, authenticity in communication is a refreshing and vital practice.

Transparent and authentic communication allows you to assess the compatibility of your values, beliefs, and goals. It provides an opportunity to explore whether your faith aligns, whether your vision for the future is in harmony, and whether you both share a similar sense of purpose.

Navigating Challenges Through Communication

Challenges are an inevitable part of any relationship. However, in "Prayerful Dating," we approach these challenges with a unique perspective. We view them as opportunities for growth and discernment. Challenges test the strength of a relationship and offer insights into whether it is in alignment with God's will.

This chapter explores how effective communication can help navigate challenges. It guides you in approaching difficult conversations with compassion, patience, and a sense of prayerful intent. It provides tools to address disagreements and conflicts in a way that respects the sacred bond of your relationship.

The Role of Prayer in Communication

Prayer remains at the heart of "Prayerful Dating," even when it comes to communication. We emphasize the practice of praying together as a way to seek God's guidance and strengthen your spiritual connection. Through shared prayers, you can explore your faith together, ask for wisdom in your relationship, and seek His blessings.

In the pages that follow, we will delve into practical exercises and strategies to enhance your communication skills and deepen your connection. "Prayerful Dating" encourages you to view communication as a way to seek God's will in your relationships, fostering a deep and meaningful connection that aligns with your faith and values.

The art of communication and connection, when approached with a prayerful heart, can transform your dating experience into a sacred journey towards love that is truly guided by God's will.

5

Nurturing a Relationship with God Together

Title: "Prayerful Dating: Seeking God's Will in Relationships"

As we journey deeper into "Prayerful Dating," we arrive at a pivotal chapter that focuses on the importance of nurturing a relationship with God together. This chapter explores the profound significance of shared faith and the ways in which it can enhance and enrich your connection with your partner.

Building a Spiritual Connection

A shared faith serves as a strong foundation upon which to build a lasting and fulfilling relationship. It offers a common language, shared values, and a framework for understanding life's complexities. In "Prayerful Dating," we place a strong emphasis on nurturing a spiritual connection as an integral part of the relationship.

This connection involves engaging in acts of worship, prayer, and contemplation together. It is about experiencing your faith as a couple, supporting each other's spiritual growth, and finding God's presence in your shared journey.

The Power of Shared Values

Your values, rooted in faith, become a guiding light in your relationship. They shape your decisions, influence your priorities, and provide a moral compass. In this chapter, we delve into the importance of identifying and discussing your shared values as a couple.

"Prayerful Dating" encourages open and honest conversations about values, beliefs, and goals. These conversations help you understand the role of faith in your relationship and how it aligns with God's will. They also provide a foundation for making important life decisions together, from daily choices to long-term commitments.

Embracing Spiritual Practices

The act of worship and spiritual practice can be a profound bonding experience for couples in "Prayerful Dating." This chapter explores the various ways in which you can incorporate prayer, meditation, scripture reading, and other spiritual rituals into your relationship.

Engaging in these practices together allows you to experience your faith in a unique and intimate way. It deepens your connection with God and with each other. It also becomes a source of strength and solace during challenging times, allowing you to lean on your faith as a couple.

Trust and Surrender

Trust and surrender are fundamental elements of "Prayerful Dating." Trust in each other and, most importantly, trust in God's plan for your relationship. Surrendering to the divine will means relinquishing control over the future and placing your faith in His guidance.

This chapter delves into the beauty of trust and surrender. It encourages you to have faith that God is actively involved in your relationship, guiding you toward His will. Trust and surrender empower you to embrace the uncertainties of the future, knowing that you are in His hands.

Serving Together

Serving others is a manifestation of faith in action. It allows you to experience the joy of giving and the fulfillment of making a positive impact on the world. This chapter explores the value of serving together as a couple.

By engaging in acts of kindness and service, you not only bond with your partner but also align your relationship with God's will. It is an embodiment of your shared faith and values in action, and it deepens the spiritual connection you have with each other.

The Role of Prayer in Your Relationship

Prayer continues to be a cornerstone of "Prayerful Dating." In this chapter, we emphasize the significance of praying together as a couple. It serves as a spiritual anchor, allowing you to seek God's guidance, wisdom, and blessings for your relationship.

Through shared prayer, you can explore your faith together, express your hopes and fears, and find solace in God's presence. It becomes a sacred practice that strengthens your connection with each other and with your Creator.

In the pages that follow, you'll find practical guidance on how to nurture a relationship with God together. "Prayerful Dating" views shared faith as a source of strength and unity, allowing you to journey toward God's will in your relationship hand in hand. The shared spiritual connection you build will not only deepen your love but also provide a firm foundation for a lasting, purposeful, and God-blessed partnership.

6

Encountering Challenges on the Path

Title: "Prayerful Dating: Seeking God's Will in Relationships"

In the course of our journey through "Prayerful Dating," we encounter the inevitable obstacles and challenges that come with any path, especially one as profound and sacred as seeking God's will in relationships. This chapter delves into the difficulties and trials that may arise during your journey and provides guidance on how to navigate them with faith and resilience.

The Role of Challenges

Challenges are not to be feared; they are to be embraced as opportunities for growth. In "Prayerful Dating," we acknowledge that challenges are a natural part of any relationship. They test our commitment, our patience, and our ability to rely on our faith.

Challenges can take various forms – from disagreements and misunderstandings to external pressures and unforeseen circumstances. This chapter encourages you to view these challenges as moments of discernment, where you can assess whether your relationship is in alignment with God's will.

Conflict Resolution with Faith

When disagreements and conflicts arise, the way you approach them can either draw you closer together or drive you apart. "Prayerful Dating" emphasizes the importance of addressing conflicts with faith.

You are encouraged to maintain open and honest communication, respecting each other's perspectives, and actively listening. More importantly, prayer should be your anchor during these challenging times. Seeking God's guidance through prayer can bring clarity, patience, and wisdom to your approach to conflict resolution, helping you find solutions that align with His will.

The Importance of Patience

Patience is a virtue that is especially important in "Prayerful Dating." It's the ability to wait for God's timing, to endure difficulties without losing hope, and to remain steadfast in your faith. In the face of challenges, patience can be your greatest ally.

This chapter explores the significance of patience in your relationship. It encourages you to trust the process, to be understanding when your partner faces their own trials, and to remain committed to your shared journey even when you encounter obstacles.

Seeking Guidance from Spiritual Mentors

Sometimes, the challenges you face may require wisdom beyond your own. In "Prayerful Dating," we recognize the value of seeking guidance from trusted spiritual mentors or advisors. These individuals can offer insights, wisdom, and perspective that can help you navigate difficult moments.

This chapter guides you on how to approach the process of seeking counsel.

It encourages you to identify mentors who share your faith and values, and who can help you understand the implications of the challenges you face in your relationship.

Trusting God's Plan

Above all, in the face of challenges, "Prayerful Dating" urges you to trust in God's plan. Challenges are not insurmountable obstacles but rather opportunities to reaffirm your faith and commitment. Trust in the divine plan, even when it seems obscure, and believe that God is guiding your relationship according to His will.

This chapter explores how trust in God's plan can provide you with the strength and resilience needed to overcome the challenges in your relationship. It reminds you that the difficulties you face are part of your journey, and they can ultimately lead you closer to God's will.

The Role of Prayer in Overcoming Challenges

Prayer remains a vital component of addressing and overcoming challenges in your relationship. By praying together and individually, you seek God's guidance and support during trying times. This chapter provides practical advice on how to incorporate prayer into your approach to challenges and make it a source of strength and comfort.

In the pages that follow, you'll find insights and strategies to navigate the challenges that may arise on your path of "Prayerful Dating." Challenges are not to be feared; they are to be embraced as opportunities for growth and discernment. With faith, patience, and trust, you can overcome these hurdles, strengthening your relationship and aligning it more closely with God's will.

7

Celebrating Love in God's Will

Title: "Prayerful Dating: Seeking God's Will in Relationships"

As we journey through "Prayerful Dating," we come to a chapter that celebrates the culmination of your efforts and commitment to seeking God's will in your relationship. This chapter focuses on the joy of love in its purest form – love that is divinely guided and spiritually enriching.

The Beauty of Alignment

Alignment with God's will is a testament to the faith, patience, and perseverance you have exhibited throughout your "Prayerful Dating" journey. It's the recognition that your relationship is in harmony with God's plan for your lives, a confirmation that you have sought His guidance and blessings.

This chapter explores the beauty of alignment. It encourages you to celebrate the fact that your relationship is not solely a product of your own desires but is also shaped by divine intervention. The joy of knowing that you are where you are meant to be is a profound and humbling experience.

CELEBRATING LOVE IN GOD'S WILL

Reflecting on the Journey

Take a moment to reflect on the journey you have undertaken in "Prayerful Dating." This chapter invites you to look back and consider the challenges you've overcome, the lessons you've learned, and the growth you've experienced. Through self-reflection, you can gain a deeper understanding of how your faith has shaped your relationship.

As you reflect, consider how you've grown individually and as a couple. What spiritual milestones have you achieved, and how has your relationship with God evolved? Acknowledge the transformation that has taken place in your hearts and souls.

Embracing God's Blessings

In "Prayerful Dating," we emphasize the importance of acknowledging and embracing God's blessings in your relationship. Recognize that the love you share is a divine gift, a reflection of God's grace in your lives. This chapter encourages you to be grateful for the love you've found and the faith that has guided you to this point.

God's blessings extend beyond your relationship and touch other areas of your life. Acknowledge the goodness that has flowed into your life as a result of your faith and trust in His will.

Renewing Your Commitment

As you celebrate the love that is in alignment with God's will, consider renewing your commitment to each other and to your faith. This chapter guides you on how to express your commitment and devotion in a way that is meaningful and in harmony with your shared values.

Renewing your commitment is not only an expression of love but also a conscious act of faith. It signifies your intention to continue to seek God's will together, to grow in your spiritual journey, and to support each other's development as individuals and as a couple.

The Role of Prayer in Celebration

Prayer remains an integral part of your celebration. In this chapter, we explore how prayer can enhance the joy and significance of celebrating love in God's will. Whether it's through gratitude, reflection, or renewing your commitment, prayer brings an added layer of depth and spiritual connection to your celebrations.

Through shared prayer, you can express your love and devotion to each other, thanking God for His guidance and blessings. You can also seek His continued support and wisdom as you move forward in your journey together.

Moving Forward with Faith

While you celebrate the love that is in alignment with God's will, remember that your journey is not static. It's a continuous process of growth, faith, and renewal. This chapter encourages you to move forward with faith, trusting that God's plan for your relationship will continue to unfold in remarkable and beautiful ways.

As you conclude your "Prayerful Dating" journey, maintain your commitment to seeking God's will and nurturing your shared faith. Know that your love is an ongoing gift, a testament to the power of faith in relationships, and a reflection of God's presence in your lives.

In the pages that follow, you'll find inspiration and guidance for celebrating the love that is rooted in God's will. Your journey, while marked by challenges and growth, ultimately leads to a celebration of love that is profound, spiritually enriching, and truly aligned with the divine plan.

8

Passing the Torch of Wisdom

Title: "Prayerful Dating: Seeking God's Will in Relationships"

As we conclude our journey through "Prayerful Dating," we arrive at a chapter that highlights the importance of passing the torch of wisdom to others. This chapter is about sharing the valuable lessons, insights, and experiences you have gained with those who may be embarking on their own journey towards love guided by faith.

The Gift of Wisdom

Wisdom is a precious gift that we acquire through our experiences, challenges, and growth. In "Prayerful Dating," the wisdom gained on your journey holds immeasurable value, not only for you and your partner but also for those who may seek to follow a similar path.

This chapter explores the significance of wisdom and how it becomes a source of guidance and inspiration for others. It encourages you to acknowledge the wisdom you have gained and to consider the ways in which you can pass it on to those who may be on the same journey.

Becoming Mentors and Guides

Becoming mentors and guides is a way to pay forward the blessings you've received. As someone who has navigated the path of "Prayerful Dating," you have a unique perspective and insight into the role of faith in relationships. This chapter delves into the idea of serving as mentors and guides for others who may seek your wisdom.

Mentorship can take various forms, from providing advice and guidance to simply being a listening ear for those who need it. Sharing your experiences and the principles of "Prayerful Dating" can help others make informed choices in their own pursuit of love in God's will.

Encouraging Faith in Relationships

In a world where dating and relationships are often seen as secular pursuits, encouraging faith in relationships is a powerful message to convey. Your journey in "Prayerful Dating" serves as a testament to the possibility of aligning your love life with your faith. This chapter guides you on how to inspire and encourage faith in relationships among those around you.

By sharing your story and the principles you've embraced, you can inspire others to embark on their own journey towards love guided by faith. You can offer hope and support to those who may have been hesitant or uncertain about the role of faith in their relationships.

Fostering a Community of Faithful Daters

This chapter also emphasizes the importance of fostering a community of faithful daters. You can play a role in bringing like-minded individuals together, providing a space for sharing experiences and wisdom. Whether through discussions, support groups, or social gatherings, you can create a community where faith and relationships intersect.

Fostering a community of faithful daters not only provides support but also opens doors for collective learning and growth. It allows individuals to share their stories, seek advice, and collectively explore the challenges and joys of seeking God's will in relationships.

The Role of Prayer in Passing the Torch

As you pass the torch of wisdom to others, prayer remains a vital aspect of the process. In this chapter, we explore how prayer can guide and enrich your efforts to inspire and support others on their journey.

Through prayer, you can seek guidance on how best to serve as a mentor or guide. You can pray for the individuals you are supporting, asking for God's blessings on their journey. You can also find solace in prayer as you navigate the challenges and responsibilities of serving as a source of wisdom and guidance.

A Legacy of Love and Faith

In "Prayerful Dating," your journey becomes part of a legacy of love and faith. The lessons you've learned, the wisdom you've gained, and the support you provide to others are all elements of this legacy. This chapter encourages you to embrace the idea that your journey contributes to a greater tapestry of love and faith that extends beyond your own relationship.

Your legacy is not just about the love you share with your partner but also the love and support you offer to others. It is a testament to the enduring power of faith in relationships and the impact it can have on individuals and communities.

In the pages that follow, you'll find guidance on how to pass the torch of wisdom to those who seek to follow in your footsteps. By sharing your experiences, embracing the role of mentorship, and fostering a community of faithful daters, you become an integral part of a legacy of love and faith that continues to inspire and guide others on their journey towards relationships aligned with God's will.

9

A Lifetime of Love and Faith

Title: "Prayerful Dating: Seeking God's Will in Relationships"

In this final chapter of "Prayerful Dating," we embrace the profound understanding that a lifetime of love and faith is the ultimate destination of our journey. This chapter explores the significance of a love that endures, and how faith remains the guiding force that sustains your relationship throughout the many seasons of life.

Love That Evolves

A love that is rooted in faith is not static; it evolves over time. As you navigate the seasons of life together, your love deepens and matures. In "Prayerful Dating," we emphasize the idea that love is not merely a fleeting emotion but a lifelong commitment to growth, mutual support, and shared values.

This chapter explores how your love can evolve in meaningful ways. It encourages you to embrace the changes and challenges that life brings, viewing them as opportunities to strengthen your bond and your faith.

Nurturing Your Faith

Faith is not a fixed state; it requires nurturing and cultivation. In your journey, it is important to remember that your faith will also evolve. This chapter delves into the ways in which you can continue to nurture your faith as a couple.

Through prayer, reflection, and shared spiritual practices, you can deepen your connection with God and with each other. Your relationship becomes a source of inspiration and growth, as you support each other in your individual spiritual journeys.

Passing Down a Legacy

Just as you have received wisdom and support from those who have gone before you, you have a responsibility to pass down your own legacy of love and faith. In "Prayerful Dating," we acknowledge the role of mentoring and guiding the next generation, as well as providing guidance and support for those who come after you.

This chapter encourages you to reflect on the legacy you wish to leave behind. It emphasizes the importance of sharing your story, your wisdom, and your experiences with others, so they too can embark on their own journey of seeking God's will in relationships.

Celebrating Milestones

As your love and faith continue to evolve, it's important to celebrate the milestones you achieve. Whether it's anniversaries, achievements, or personal and spiritual growth, acknowledging these moments is a way to recognize the progress you've made.

In "Prayerful Dating," we encourage you to celebrate these milestones with gratitude and prayer. Reflect on the journey you've undertaken, express your thanks to God, and seek His blessings for the path that lies ahead.

Prayer as a Lifelong Companion

Throughout your journey in "Prayerful Dating," prayer has been a constant companion. It remains a source of strength and guidance as you navigate the seasons of life together. This chapter explores the enduring role of prayer in your relationship.

Prayer provides solace during difficult times, offers gratitude during moments of joy, and seeks wisdom in the face of challenges. As you embrace a lifetime of love and faith, prayer remains a central practice that keeps you connected to God and to each other.

A Lifetime of Love and Faith

In the pages that follow, you'll find guidance on how to embrace a lifetime of love and faith. Your journey through "Prayerful Dating" serves as a foundation for a relationship that is not only rooted in God's will but is also a source of endless love, growth, and spiritual enrichment.

A lifetime of love and faith is not without its trials and tribulations, but it is marked by a deep and abiding connection with your Creator and your partner. It is a testament to the enduring power of faith in relationships and the impact it can have on your life's journey.

10

The Journey Continues

Title: "Prayerful Dating: Seeking God's Will in Relationships"

In this final chapter of "Prayerful Dating," we embark on a new beginning, embracing the concept that the journey never truly ends. The path to seeking God's will in relationships is an ongoing one, filled with learning, growth, and the ever-deepening connection to your faith.

A Forever Journey

The journey of "Prayerful Dating" is not confined to a specific period of your life; it's a lifelong endeavor. This chapter underscores the idea that as you continue in your relationship, your faith, and your journey toward God's will, there will always be new experiences, challenges, and opportunities for growth.

Your commitment to faith and prayer remains an enduring foundation that will guide you through the changing seasons of life. Embrace the realization that the journey continues, and it is a path you walk together.

Learning and Evolving

As you move forward in your relationship, remember that you are in a state of perpetual learning and evolution. "Prayerful Dating" encourages you to remain open to new insights, to seek wisdom from your experiences, and to adapt as you grow individually and as a couple.

In this chapter, we explore the importance of maintaining a growth mindset. The ability to learn and evolve together strengthens your bond and ensures that your relationship remains in alignment with God's will.

Sharing Your Journey

Your journey is not solely for your benefit; it is also an opportunity to share your story with others. The experiences, wisdom, and faith you've gained can serve as inspiration and guidance for those who may be on their own path to seeking God's will in relationships.

This chapter encourages you to consider how you can continue to pass on the torch of wisdom to others, just as you received guidance and support from those who came before you. Whether through mentorship, storytelling, or community involvement, your journey can inspire others in their pursuit of faith-based love.

Embracing New Beginnings

Each new day is a new beginning, and "Prayerful Dating" reminds you to embrace these fresh starts with open hearts. Your relationship is a dynamic and evolving entity, and with each new day, you have the opportunity to reaffirm your commitment to faith and love.

In this chapter, we delve into the beauty of new beginnings. We encourage you to approach each day as a chance to deepen your connection with God and with your partner. Your relationship is not confined by the past but is continuously enriched by the choices you make today.

The Role of Prayer in Continuing the Journey

Prayer remains the thread that weaves through your journey, no matter how far you've come. In this chapter, we explore how prayer continues to be a vital part of your ongoing journey. Whether in moments of gratitude, reflection, or seeking guidance, prayer remains your constant companion.

Through prayer, you can find strength, solace, and wisdom as you face the future. It connects you to your Creator and to each other, ensuring that your journey is guided by faith and love.

A Lifelong Adventure

In "Prayerful Dating," you have embarked on a lifelong adventure that embraces faith, love, and a commitment to seeking God's will in your relationship. This chapter serves as a reminder that the journey is an ongoing and evolving experience, rich with the promise of continued growth and spiritual enrichment.

As you move forward, continue to cultivate your faith, deepen your love, and share your wisdom with others. Embrace each new day as a chance to reaffirm your commitment to your faith, your partner, and your Creator. Your "Prayerful Dating" journey has brought you to this point, and it is just the beginning of a lifelong adventure of love and faith.

11

A Love Story Written by God

Title: "Prayerful Dating: Seeking God's Will in Relationships"

In the grand narrative of "Prayerful Dating," we arrive at a chapter that acknowledges the profound and beautifully complex love story written by God. This chapter explores the idea that our journey in seeking God's will in relationships is ultimately a testament to divine intervention and the divine authorship of our love stories.

Divine Authorship

In "Prayerful Dating," we emphasize that our relationships are not solely of our own making but are co-authored by God. This chapter delves into the concept of divine authorship, where God is the master storyteller, crafting our love stories with care and purpose.

Recognizing divine authorship means that every aspect of your relationship, from your initial meeting to your shared experiences, has a unique place in the narrative of your love story. It's the acknowledgment that God's hand is at work, guiding and shaping your journey.

The Beauty of God's Timing

Timing plays a crucial role in love stories authored by God. In "Prayerful Dating," we acknowledge that the moments when you meet, the challenges you face, and the milestones you celebrate are all part of God's perfect timing. This chapter explores the beauty of trusting in God's timing.

By embracing God's timing, you can find solace in the waiting, strength in the patience, and gratitude in the moments of connection. You understand that every twist and turn in your relationship is a piece of the larger love story that God is weaving.

Lessons in the Unexpected

Many love stories have unexpected twists and turns, and in "Prayerful Dating," we view the unexpected as opportunities for growth and discernment. This chapter encourages you to appreciate the lessons in the unexpected, recognizing that God often speaks to us through the surprises in our relationships.

Unforeseen challenges and surprises become moments of reflection and learning, helping you navigate your relationship with a deeper understanding of God's will. By embracing the unexpected, you become open to the wisdom that God imparts through these experiences.

The Power of Faith

Faith is a central theme in "Prayerful Dating," and it remains a powerful force in love stories written by God. Your faith is not just an aspect of your relationship; it's the fuel that drives your love story. This chapter explores how faith is not just a backdrop but an active and guiding presence.

Your faith is what leads you to seek God's will, to navigate challenges, and to celebrate your love with gratitude. It's the enduring foundation upon which your love story is built, and it infuses your relationship with purpose and meaning.

The Role of Prayer in the Love Story

Prayer remains at the heart of your love story, serving as a constant dialogue with God throughout your journey. This chapter emphasizes the role of prayer in your love story, providing guidance, support, and connection to the divine.

Through prayer, you express your gratitude for the love you've found, seek God's guidance for the future, and find comfort in moments of difficulty. It is the thread that weaves through the pages of your love story, connecting you to God's will and to each other.

A Love Story That Inspires

In the pages that follow, you'll find inspiration and guidance for embracing your love story written by God. It is a story of faith, love, and purpose, guided by divine authorship and written with the pen of your experiences, challenges, and growth.

Your love story is not just for you; it's a narrative that can inspire and guide others on their own journeys. By recognizing God's hand in your relationship, trusting in His timing, and embracing the unexpected, you become a living testament to the beauty of a love story authored by God.

12

A Lifetime of Gratitude

Title: "Prayerful Dating: Seeking God's Will in Relationships"

In this final chapter of "Prayerful Dating," we explore the profound sense of gratitude that accompanies a journey deeply rooted in faith and love. It is a chapter that reflects on the blessings and the lessons learned, and it encourages you to cultivate a lifelong attitude of gratitude.

The Gift of Love

Your journey in "Prayerful Dating" is a testament to the gift of love. Love that is not just of human making, but divinely guided and nurtured. This chapter celebrates the love that you have found, and it encourages you to express gratitude for the love that has enriched your life.

Love, as a gift, reminds you of the beauty and the depth of God's love. It prompts you to give thanks for the love you've been blessed with and to express that gratitude through your actions and words.

Embracing Life's Lessons

Life's lessons are woven throughout your journey in "Prayerful Dating." From the challenges that have tested your faith to the moments of joy that have deepened your connection, these lessons serve as signposts along your path.

This chapter encourages you to embrace these lessons with gratitude. They are the building blocks of your relationship, shaping your faith and your love. Through reflection and gratitude, you can find meaning in the difficulties and insights in the triumphs.

The Beauty of Faith

Faith is a cornerstone of "Prayerful Dating," and this chapter underscores the beauty of faith. It encourages you to be thankful for the faith that has guided your journey, nurtured your love, and enriched your relationship.

Faith brings hope, strength, and purpose to your love story. It serves as a source of guidance in seeking God's will, and it deepens your connection with your partner and your Creator. Expressing gratitude for your faith deepens your relationship with God and with each other.

Prayer as an Act of Gratitude

Throughout your journey, prayer has been an integral practice. This chapter explores the role of prayer as an act of gratitude. It encourages you to offer prayers of thanksgiving for the love you've found, the faith that sustains you, and the blessings that have enriched your life.

By expressing gratitude through prayer, you align your hearts and your relationship with a sense of humble appreciation. It becomes a reminder of God's constant presence in your lives and a source of comfort during moments of reflection.

Serving as a Source of Inspiration

In "Prayerful Dating," your journey serves as an inspiration for others who seek faith-based love. This chapter invites you to express gratitude for the opportunity to inspire and guide others on their own journeys.

Through your story, your wisdom, and your example, you have the power to encourage others to seek God's will in their relationships. Expressing gratitude for this role affirms the impact and purpose of your journey.

A Lifetime of Gratitude

A lifetime of gratitude is a perspective that views every day, every experience, and every challenge as a gift. It is a way of embracing your relationship, your faith, and your journey in "Prayerful Dating" with a profound sense of thankfulness.

In the pages that follow, you'll find guidance on how to cultivate a lifetime of gratitude. Your journey is not just about seeking God's will but also about celebrating the love, faith, and wisdom that have enriched your life. Through gratitude, you deepen your connection with God and with each other, recognizing the blessings that are woven throughout your relationship.

Book Summary: Prayerful Dating - Seeking God's Will in Relationships

"Prayerful Dating: Seeking God's Will in Relationships" is a profound and inspirational guide that explores the intersection of faith and romantic relationships. In this enlightening book, readers embark on a journey that emphasizes the importance of aligning their love lives with their faith, nurturing a relationship with God, and seeking divine guidance throughout their romantic journey.

The book is divided into twelve chapters, each addressing critical aspects of faith-based dating and relationships, with a focus on God's will as the guiding force:

1. Starting with Faith: The journey begins with an exploration of the foundational role of faith in relationships. It emphasizes the significance of seeking God's will as a couple.

2. The Power of Prayer: Chapter 2 delves into the transformative power of prayer in romantic relationships. It highlights the importance of turning to God for guidance and wisdom.

3. Understanding God's Will: This chapter provides insights into discerning God's will in relationships, navigating challenges, and making decisions in accordance with faith.

4. Building a Strong Foundation: Readers discover the necessity of establishing a solid foundation of shared values and principles that align with their faith.

5. Nurturing a Relationship with God Together: Chapter 5 explores the beauty of nurturing a shared spiritual connection, emphasizing the importance of faith in daily life.

6. Encountering Challenges on the Path: Relationships inevitably face challenges, and this chapter offers guidance on navigating these obstacles with faith, trust, and prayer.

7. Celebrating Love in God's Will: Readers are encouraged to celebrate the love that is divinely guided, marked by gratitude and a deep spiritual connection.

8. Passing the Torch of Wisdom: Chapter 8 focuses on the importance of mentoring and guiding others on their own faith-based dating journeys.

9. A Lifetime of Love and Faith: This chapter emphasizes that the journey is lifelong and explores the concept of enduring love guided by faith.

10. The Journey Continues: Readers are reminded that the journey never truly ends and that their relationship, faith, and love continue to evolve.

11. A Love Story Written by God: The penultimate chapter delves into the idea that our love stories are authored by God, guided by divine timing and faith.

12. A Lifetime of Gratitude: The final chapter encourages readers to cultivate a lifelong attitude of gratitude for the love, faith, and wisdom they have found throughout their journey.

"Prayerful Dating" offers practical advice, heartfelt stories, and deep spiritual insights, making it a comprehensive guide for those seeking to intertwine their faith with their romantic lives. It teaches that a relationship grounded in faith, nurtured through prayer, and guided by God's will can be a profoundly fulfilling and enriching journey. Readers are encouraged to embrace each day as a gift, a new beginning in their love story written by God, and to cultivate a sense of gratitude for the blessings they've received.

www.ingramcontent.com/pod-product-compliance
Lightning Source LLC
LaVergne TN
LVHW010438070526
838199LV00066B/6076